Live Canon
2021 Anthology

First Published in 2021
By Live Canon Ltd
www.livecanon.co.uk

All rights reserved

© Live Canon 2021

978-1-909703-86-5

A CIP catalogue record for this book is available from the British Library.

Live Canon
2021 Anthology

The poems in this anthology were longlisted for the
2021 Live Canon International Poetry Prize

Contents

In an Empty Train
Antony Mair

I sit with my bag beside me – my favourite one,
bought in Venice: olive green, cream stitching.
The leather's from cattle, who conspire, it's said,
to destroy us, in several decades' time. Outside,
the fields they graze in blur in the evening light.
Oaktrees darken against a blood-red sky.

I'm masked against infection – an invisible threat
happening, like so much else significant,
beyond my sight, in some ultraviolet space.
I've been here before – the night I saw dark patches
on my lover's skin, and knew he'd die; the day
a few weeks later, when my test showed negative.

I wondered then why the fates took him, left me -
legacies of actions as casual as my purchase,
in that scented clutter by the gondolas,
of the bag at my side. The train hurtles on
through countryside we walked in, onwards
into the night. I sit and wait.

28 trailers
Sarah Terkaoui

twenty eight refrigerated trailers
in the hospital car park

filled methodically
by shell shocked
administrators and audiologists

and secretaries who never
thought they would wear
sweat slicked protective suits

that hardly hide their fear
while ambulance staff
in squat yellow queues

speak to each other
in numbers and stats
and tell patients

lie still, try to take
proper breaths,
while they wait

their turns
for small cubicles
hurriedly scrubbed

beneath white harsh lights
behind thin green curtains
where someone else like them

lay down for the first time
and the last time
tell them not to move

so they can be monitored
and pictures taken
to be read like books

that start at the end
and forget there ever was
a beginning

but mostly so they never see
what sits in the hospital car park

Two hundred and sixty feet
David Underdown

Over the years there must have been hundreds
but the one I saw, just one thank god, lives on
in mental debris trawled up today
by no more than a few words from a book.
She lies still where she fell
on that morning I saw her sprawled
across the mud of the retreating tide.

Spreadeagled, legs all wrong, her body
harnessed gravity but lost its proper shape.
At thirty-two feet per second per second
she fell through half a furlong of air.
Think of it in cricket pitches or the breadth of motorways.
Think how ground sped up as she dropped
past wooded cliffs and hulks of boats.

Looking down, her arms outstretched
as if to save herself, she would not see
Brunel's fine towers framed against the sky.
Did she hesitate? Was there a hopeless cry
for help that did not come, or was her short flight
silent, like a photograph, black and white
and never in the family album?

She was the first dead body I had seen
and half a lifetime later I am hoping
I am not the only one to wonder;
whether in a quiet moment
there is someone to imagine
the grandchildren who never came.
Or telling a child *you had an auntie once.*

A Baby Speaks on his Birthday in an Autumn Garden, 2020
Josephine Corcoran

It's the equinox, time for a cake and candle –
your first – although we're not allowed to be with you.
Instead, we hold you in our kitchens like a lantern,
your face inside our phones, small bringer of light.
For half your life, your world
has been your Mum and Dad,
house, garden, local street. You know
nothing, yet, of your big extended family.

Look at the colours, Sweetheart!
Your Mum films you scrambling into autumn,
leaves sparking orange, parched as kindle,
scratch and crackle through your knees and hands.
None of us understand this virus, shaken loose
from burning forests. Denial breathes inside our masks
and you make gentle sounds for each twig, branch,
root and leaf you honour with your deep attention.

What a garden! someone says, in lieu of counting
the daily deaths. Fizzing with energy,
you raise both arms, spilling autumn towards
cousins, aunties, uncles – words you've never heard –
our voices calling through the universe
of flaming creepers, burnt gold berries, scorched
tangle of vines blazing on fences, roses faded
as if kissed with soot. We hear you telling us to *Look!*

A Small House on Higher Ground
Colin Watts

It feels good to ease out of my survival suit
and stretch out on the sofa. I check the seals
around the windows and front and back doors,
reckon I can turn off the air-con for long enough
to bring a little silence to my soul, though of course
the CO2 monitor can bring that crashing down.

Always assuming it's powered up. After months
of heavy rain the solar panels scarcely generate
enough to turn on a light, let alone boil a kettle.
I don't think I'll need heating, though you can't be
certain, now that even high-tech forecasting can't
keep pace with the vagaries of our weather.

Now that pre-recording is illegal and ad-watching
mandatory, I search out pirate channels. I dare
not turn off Mainstream for too long and the Love
Thy Neighbour system is lucrative enough
for even decent folk to succumb. My current
favourite is New Atlantis, an unofficial IndieDoc.

Divers evade the armed coastguard patrols and take us
through submerged seaside towns like Blackpool
and Margate, filming the tide turning the big wheels
and riding bareback on the rotting horses. Very soon
they will be captured and humiliated and their
programmes deleted. Meanwhile, I am thankful.

I think of the undrowned languishing in makeshift
so-called Rescue Centres on barren hillsides and thank
my lucky stars for a small house on higher ground.
I try hard to mourn the many thousands taken
by the waves, whose bodies were never recovered,
but find the words of grief I have are not enough.

Every night my sleep is shattered by fierce dreams
of the poisoned air and bitter wars that engulf
our dying world. I am trapped in underground caves,
waters rising to my neck, or choking on my own
doorstep, unable to find my keys. I wake sweating,
heart pounding. I check the windows and the doors.

After the Asylum
Chaucer Cameron

she took up ornithology, collected
feathers from the red-throated loon,

studied them obsessively then hurried
to the water, spat secrets, contours, down.

Her interests were in feathers, sunlight and water
continuous movement helped to keep her calm.

Sometimes there were moments she slipped
back to broken, a dry river kind of broken.

Hey, river, river there's nowhere else to go,
gone, gone, quietly tomorrow.

When tomorrow came, all her eggs were taken
she was found on the road, her red throat wide open.

Archaeology
P.N. Singer

Finger the pages of the books you read;
visit the less lost person;
find that the stones stand and the streets have light
and life as always fades ruined in sun
in forgotten loved corners,
of coffee and stupid clarity;

and find no words to tell
how much is frosted about this peculiar lost heart,
or what it lost,
or that two persons, fabulous, close,
are nowhere now to touch,
or that this other life could have been yours, supposedly,
or what that means
to you, or to it,
and to everything in between.

Unhappiness, cold digger.

Cornish Morning
Vanessa Lampert

Now blooming pink puffs of thrift, and puffs
of lilac scabious wander over the cliff path.
Now sea campion and celandine, now sun
gilds this morning ruthless bright. No sadness
has followed us here this time, no loss,
so we walk where a skylark hangs his song
above a gulley where a shipwreck rusts,
no life was lost, and the gorse sings fierce
of yellow. A cloud of migrant wheatears
alights in a field by the path. Now the pale
aquamarine sea, now black lichen and green
grow on granite. Now warbler and chough
trust their wings to the roughshod wind. It's enough.
Today there's nothing left for us to mourn.

Bert Jarman at the Pentre
Chris Hardy

At eight am he comes from the milking parlour,
blue overalls stained to the knees,
buttons open over his thick wool cardigan,
bringing into the kitchen a fog
of sour milk, silage, diesel, manure
and Old Holborn rolled in liquorice paper.
His father sitting by the range asks
how the morning is then turns back
to telling how he survived Gallipoli,
while Sioned cracks eggs in bacon fat,
adds sliced bread to the pan and a black
puck of pig's blood speckled white.

I'd walk to the farm carrying a bucket
for our yellow morning milk warm from the tank
as the cows were turning out, with Meadow Ned,
a dark red, low-slung Hereford bull
ambling behind, marble locks shining
in the sun, dewlap dragging on the grass
as he lowered his head to savour through
gaping nostrils and dripping lips the fumes
beneath his harem's lifting tails.
Sometimes he'd wait by our gate, sawing his jaw
along the top bar, rumbling like a tiger,
blowing saliva and hay-sweet humid breath.

Scratching his granite brow I wondered
if it was safe to lift the latch and walk
as Bert had said it was after it took
four of us hanging on a bull-staff
to stop Ned killing a young Holstein
that broke a hedge to reach the herd.

We slowed him so the piebald bull could run
from the simmering lake of scent pooled
above the pasture where the cows filled bellies,
udders swollen and drooping down,
hung from jutting hips, spines, shoulders,
a cart of bones inside their skins.

Blackspot
Mary-Jane Holmes

"In compliance with the requirements of sections 45 to 50 of the Communication Act 2003, as appropriate and relevant to the proposal, the Universal Service Provider ([British Telecommunications plc / Kingston Communications (Hull) plc) will not remove the public phone box at Nettlepot, Lunedale, if at least one phone call is made from the location within a 12-month period."

Although the man from the Parish Council called it
pro-active, on a day like this, cowslips buttering
the ground, colostrum rising in the fields, it feels
more like pilgrimage to walk this offering of coins
to the phone box beneath Whyte's Hill nestled
like a roadside hermitage in this land devoid
of radio signals: no 4G (or 3 or 2), no roaming
networks or wireless carriers, just this booth,
algae-streaked, strip-lit, its fish tank fluorescence
a monstrance of hope to the broken-down, the lost.
Inside, it is wilderness that finds refuge in this kiosk:
keypad - a quire of moss, coin return - a robin's nest,
which makes it all the more miraculous to lift
the handset etched with lichen from its cradle-hook,
hear the crackling dial tone, its static - a reliquary
of all things analogue – the speaking clock, party line
gossip, the compassion of charges reversed,
and the sudden knowledge that the only numbers
I'm able to recall off the top of my head, preserved
like poems or songs rote-learned, belong to childhood
or the dead. Grandparents, father, brother and that boy
I never told how I felt (not pro-active enough) who
promised to call and never did while I sat for hours
on the stairs in the hall where the telephone lived,
learning to map the blackspots in that country called love.

Bread
John Kefala Kerr

We spoke of nothing else that day:
of crocodiles, meteorites and fossils.

My mother even telephoned to say
how much she enjoyed every mouthful.

While sawing through the prehistoric crust,
we bemoaned modernity and complained of

how backward we all are now compared to then.
Hours passed with that "thing called bread"

reducing our table manners to the gnawing
of the impoverished, and even at night when lying

un-buttered, un-delivered to our bed with exquisite
inappropriateness, it still made crumbs of us.

Crazy Mad Bastard
Tim Relf

I see my old buddy on Zoom: Aberdeen,
he's in, but more than merely distance and digital delay between us.
It's as if he's pondering a different question:
One from before the quiz started
or one yet to come.

I try not to stare at him,
this middle-age man in a one-sixth segment of the screen, hanging
on to a chair in his mum's house.
Zoom shares rocket, he says, his hands working the handles.
That's right, Simon, one of the five replies.

Hey, Jenks, I ask – remember the Alisons? But my words disappear
down the cracks between the boxes
and the quiz questions move on.

Gardening.
Gardening.

That was when you had hair, mate, I say, digging,
but what I'm really thinking is:
Before you quit college
or got in your car one Wednesday and drove to Scotland
or all the other things in-between.

What popular perennial has the Latin name digitalis?
What popular perennial has the Latin name digitalis?

This was the guy who once dated three Alisons in a year and now he's 51 and
   niggling at the wood on the arm of a chair with a nail as if he's trying to
   scratch off a splash of paint.

Did you hear I'm in Scotland? he asks.
I'd heard you'd gone nuts again, I say.

I went...

Your internet connection is unstable
Your internet connection is unstable

... we sit for a while, my wife and I, holding hands
and when we get back online, the squares on the screen have moved and
    everyone other than Jenks has moved within them too: shifted positions
    on sofas, kids have joined, drinks have been topped up, the film round is
    nearly done.

This is what his life must be like:
Coming back to find everyone else still there,
laughing and holding hands and the questions asked.

We might have missed the film round, but he missed a whole batch of the
    early weddings, the 30ths, a three-year chunk somewhere this side of 40 –
not at his mum's in Scotland, but somewhere not so very different to there:
    a room, someone else's place, overwhelmed.

And I'm remembering how once in the expansive, emboldened heart of a
    four-year good spell,
this man told me the worst thing was when people treated him differently.
Promise me you'll never stop taking the piss out of me, he'd said –
at that moment, the past and future barely shadows in his periphery vision.
If I'm behaving like a crazy mad bastard, you will tell me, won't you, he'd said.
Promise me that.
Please.

Famous dogs.
Famous dogs.

Three times a question about a *Blue Peter* dog is asked.
Three times my old buddy, hanging on to a chair in his mum's house, says:
    Foxglove.

I so wanted him to be more than this –
the so-much-less-than-one-sixth-of-a-screen this crazy mad bastard is today.

Dark river
Mark Huband

Moon swabs that imagined epitaph, told
in a folded knot of sheets. Twilight passed
as dusk, as the place come from, as the place to hold away
from the window where the light is cast
upon all that is unseen. Hide it now.
There may be time to share all you carry
from the cradle day. The night winds blow
like mirrors to the shift of time. Hurry.
The hour perhaps is ripe with wounds to heal
by the kiss of lips on a bed of steel
carved from skein skin wet as a seep of blood
warm as the cock you mould now in your hands.
Our star is where the comet once scud
to where our ocean tears the desert lands.

This street is only its reminiscence.
A road. The road scarred. A step was taken
like a promise woken onto silence
that is the distance of what's forsaken
when the blood has spoken. There is no road.
Nothing passed along the way to here,
where the hot of heat of fire glowed gold.
This street, this road leads far away to where
a sand grain wombs the jagged oyster shell.
Dream in hot sweat. Night clouds cast moonlight's spell
among the bluebells. There was no story,
until some time passed and something happened
that had no past the night could carry
into the room your cold hands opened.

She you him me they we. They are two
among within upon the beats of hearts.
Hearts beat to the clatter of wings that flew

from the nursery tales where the timescape starts
among strewn shards. A cut glass sky dispersed.
Dark river dark river shoulder your moon
through the marsh twilight that quenches your thirst.
She. Him. They lick salt from the old brass spoon,
the one she carried over the page
into the image she stole of her age.
He. She. He hears all the voices said
of time in hands wrung as knots of water
drowned as gasped throats rinsed parched by the dead, the
dead who follow this son and daughter.

This street is only its last circumstance,
its final prediction remembered lost.
She. He. They moon-eye linger the barbed fence,
a walled frontier where their futures crossed.
Just circumstance at a nameless border.
Moon. Sun. That self-same moon. That self-same sun,
dayless nightless where the river's wider
than ocean's depthless imagination
flooding their cavernous circumstance.
He. She. There. There are the shoals to balance
on the tips of tongues where coarse fingers play
to the mouth of promise, the whispered word
a myth told tell on a lost winter's day,
when the child within was at last heard.

Bone frames a skin wrapped in laughter's promise
of scented joy. Once ageless. Once timeless
as breath to lips to kiss. As lips that kiss,
as words that carve sweet breath from those places
where molten rivers foam their ecstasy.
Like nothing. Like nothing, but loneliness
and aftermath all broken, mystery
unspoken, crass moments struck wordless
as a fading fire of breath and skin
and muscle limbs to wrap a heaven in.

Gone among the sleepers now. All sleeping,
the bodies sing of regeneration,
night passed, its lush moments slowly seeping
into the dawn light's tongue-tied stagnation.

Skin now taut as a painter's gaping canvas
frames his hollow light upon an easel.
Carve colour. Twist. Gnarl life from dowsed embers
fanned to flames in shadows soft as pastel.
Make face. Make hands. Make fine body. Make all
that cannot hope to be the one it is.
It looks back at you, answering your call
as if your craft had borne your fantasies.
It shapes naked at your touch, dark river
pouring the shoals as your portraits gather.
Now it is yours, its veins a knotted forest
howling empty words into the hollow
night your hands have crafted from the secrets
hidden in the faces you now follow.

You saw him naked, cast in honey sun,
and conjured him the morning he would leave,
then sugared the milken seed of him
and sewed the gilded mantel that you weave
beneath the fig tree by the river home
near the Corsair's castle wall. The story
might have opened of what might once become
if the river had carried them to sea.
But you lay entwined by the beat of hearts,
as stone hooves dragged the apple carts
beneath an open window. A hollow
body wanders that shadow castle street,
a pillow aching tears, as his footsteps slow
to the pace of oceans at his feet.

Dear Bees –
Emma Simon

I know it's a lot to bear,
these half-voiced mumblings and frets
among the budding lavender.
It's not as if you haven't got
your own troubles to worry about,
but here I go, trowel in hand,
making heavy work of the weeds.
I'm no longer sure if I'm digging up
dandelions or anemones.
Listen, the news isn't good today
but I guess you knew that,
bumbling stalk to stalk, garden to garden
to the frazzled hums
of one more disappointment.
Do we weigh down your wings
with all these confessions?
Secrets charging your cells like batteries,
gossipy snippets stuck to your legs
as you rise from the buddleia.
We unburden ourselves to an afternoon sky,
our little striped consciences.
Look at them fly. Through the fence I saw
a woman next door kneel down by the border,
the sound of her prayers
drowned out by the continual loops
of the lawn sprinkler.

Doves
Isabella Mead

- a typeface reserved for elevated words:
for *In the beginning there was the Word,*
for *Paradise Lost,* for *Crossing the Bar,*

for marks on vellum in golden edging;
echoes of Venice, the flourishes of serif
on chic slanted letters, petite and compressed,

rippled with curlicues, with flicks and finesse:
poised figures curling the little finger
to sip from a teacup or cocktail glass;

these delicate characters, on tiny block-punches,
the centre of a resented inheritance case,
made a man walk the dark London mist

for one hundred nights, his silhouette
releasing sack after sack from Hammersmith Bridge;
each fall abrupt as a shot collared dove

till a ton of stencils on pieces of metal
had sunk to the depths of the Thames. They rested,
splintered amongst rusted coins and bottles.

A search started up one hundred years later
as a typesetter longed to discover the secrets,
the sweeps of serif, the traces of Venice.

The first letter the divers found was a *V,*
for victory, for peace, or else: Leave us be,
we are suited here, half-submerged in silt,

in this river that swallowed the *HMS London*,
the *Princess Alice* and the *Marchioness,*
and all the figures, unwritten, unfinished,

with their coiffed hair, eyeliner flicks and finesse,
who curled little fingers when lifting a glass,
who lost a paradise, crossing the bar.

Edvard Munch in Havordfordwest

Pam Thompson

Easter Saturday, his type of weather—
squally, grey. He wanders up the High Street,

buys a cagoule and a flask from the Army and Navy,
considers a Magilux torch but puts it back.

WH Smiths are giving away Cadburys mini-eggs
with the *Daily Mail*. He queues for ages.

The man behind the till insists he *must* take
this newspaper and not the one he prefers.

Three young women with piercings in their faces
are leaning against the railing outside Tesco—

one has sea -green hair. When he paints her
he'll make the colours vibrate until you can hear them.

He buys tomatoes and crusty bread.
As she fills the flask, the woman in Greggs

seems to understand what he says to her in Norwegian.
On St Mary's Bridge he has some sort of turn

that history will repeat— on pub signs, posters,
as though all the portraits of his homeland,

of his sister on her sickbed, never happened,
but it passes and the world stays still again.

This morning, it's all the time it takes to feed ducks
on the river and pour coffee from a blue enamel flask.

Extinction Events
David Bleiman

There's sun and birds and blossom here,
clean air, enough to drink,
but to me this is a *goodly prison*.
We clap for our carers
and tap on the plumbing
to a man in a neighbouring cell,
who scratches the days
of a five-bar gate
on his living room wall.

And oh, last spring in Chicago,
the Loop and the Lake and the jazz,
sipping cocktails
to scrape the sky.
My exuberant trainers
let in the rain
on the way to the Field Museum.

So distant now, it feels Cretaceous,
not even us, not us at all but
deep bone time,
accessible by excavation.
Someone slightly familiar,
classified as female by the pelvis,
sees a gift shop lurking
behind the titanosaur.
'They surely sell socks', says she.

And oh, the world they ruled
will never be the same.
Feet dry now, confined, I like to wear
those dinosaur socks,
soft slippers,
sink into beer,
skip over sticky sentiments.

Factors which Contraindicate a Diagnosis
Katharine Goda

Be sectioned or go voluntarily.
She should / should not believe them.

In dreams of escape she takes / leaves the buggy.
She does / does not love this baby.

When she tries to run from the weight
they notice / don't notice her heartrate.

The ECG finds anomalies.
She doesn't care / is worried.

Asking for help is rarely / never easy.
Inadequate trust / tends toward dependency.

Voices pertain to early ordeals / keen grip of psychiatry.
They find some labels. She feels / doesn't feel seen.

She means / doesn't mean
to swerve in front of the lorry.

Genealogy
Ralph La Rosa

It happens lately as he's walking,
when simple sounds will tip his balance:
a distant child's bright morning laughter,
a maker's rapid hammer strikes,
a woman's song that rhymes *forever*,
the echoing cries that wet his eyes
when unseen children head for home.
Beneath the rustling winds in trees,
he shuffles cautiously, crunching
fallen leaves before his house.
Inside, he struggles and finds sleep,
but in a windswept dream he's drifting
from his thinning family tree,
drops spinning like a dried-out leaf.

Gravity rules
Eva Hilberg

Once a day, blow your mind,
and let the apple drop.

Disintegrate this table
to molecules, with your thoughts,

feel the charge that runs
through each tiny orbit,

each piece in its place
positioned in a planetary grid

of protonic constellations,
spinning slowly on its side.

Just think, what is up
may actually be down, or all around,

compacted by constant movement
gathering and fleeing its core.

From the centre of this spin
a table top is not up, but an outside of being

in a hostile space, expanding constantly,
where mass is time, and time is distance.

This table's solid grain then
a result of planetary positioning,

the wood's roughened structure
a collection of charged cells, channelling water,

water an assemblage of charged molecules,
gases turned shapes made of extra-terrestrial dust, they suspect.

Once a day, remember gravity,
know why your cup can rest.

A table makes no sense
without the most meta of physics – remember that,

and see its wonders all around
in this weighted world.

How Much Rain Can A Cloud Hold?
Laurie Bolger

1.

When you find out it's cancer
the rosy hospital porter hands you
a bowl of stewed plums;

nobody goes without desert.

We sit in the upstairs room
me, you, the hospital porter, the trolley.
I expect you just want to get home now don't you?

Yes, I do really.

2.

Two weeks ago you cooked us beef in cherries.
Sat on the kitchen counter top
we all agreed it was cramps.

3.

When everyone's in bed
        I smoke loads

I want the sky to know
        it should be me.

On the cartoon rope bridge
I jump in front of everyone
                and save the day.

You are thirty one and look like me.

The garden pond is holding its breath
        one orange fish lurking in the green.

4.

You always feel better for a shower;
                we sit in a place we'd never usually sit
                    both brush our teeth —

I ask what you want
you smile through the froth; *a coffee and a fry up*

        but your stomach is like stones.

5.

We tell you to take a hammer
to the old Hi-Fi on the drive
to beat the shit out of it and never mind the neighbours.

You scream at steps that you can't climb.

You say *it's no good us all sitting around*

you send us out dog walking —
your brother's face scrunches up like it always will
                just before he cries —

I say: *I don't know who's running more, the dogs*
                        or our noses?

6.

I'll find you
in a house
with no windows —

the whole place
will flash blue —

I'll walk the patio steps
in the half light of December

he'll think
that I'm your ghost.

7.

I'm not watching the fish
I'm watching his hand
            on your back
            leading you from bench,
            to back door,
            then back again —

you both sit down.

8.

The first time we met
you let us have our coffees for free
I knew you were worried you'd get the sack.

The second time
you were eating sea bass
in Yum Yum Thai — blue hat.

The third time was the flat
where everyone lived once
you made us smell these cones of purple flowers.

We threw them in.

9.

I think she misses you the most,
her feet like keys over the tiles

no guests, no tissues or tea
she catches our flood in soft ears,
looks up as if to say *I'm here.*

10.

The apple juice never gets finished
so when I see the carton in the supermarket,
one green apple snatches the breath from me.

11.

I've been holding
your brother
to my chest
like glass,

on the sofa,
in the petrol garage
a damp field.

I always pick
the wrong film
we stay up crying.

On holiday
every palm tree
is an argument.

I try to post our grief
in an envelope
it's too heavy

I find you
in a book
I put you back.

12.

You tell me that you're fine
when even the air is blue

your eyes are so bright
they're just glittering!

     Raindrops hit grass
     spiders web, fizzy dew —

     you take something with you
          leaving us in all this blue.

I have paid the price for eating snow
Sarah Doyle

as a child although I could not know
it at the time. How delicious water
tasted in its crystalline form, how
thrillingly illicit the soft crunch
and slow dissolve of icy stars
yielding their structures to the heat
of my mouth. Scooped from roofs
of silenced cars or captured
on ludicrously outstretched tongue,
I have swallowed constellations
of symmetry, each its own frozen
handprint, turning my insides
bluer than I knew, incubating
winter in veins and arteries, until
now: snow falls, and snow calls
to snow, a spontaneous re-forming
of plate and needle reversing
a thousand tiny thaws, and I slow
irretrievably to sub-zero, hardened
and glacial. Snow calls to snow.

I'm afraid of the ghost of Egas Moniz
Jane Burn

I   hate my mouth. How many times have I been
in   convenient? Every moment is a wall. What on Earth did I say
tod   ay? My tongue is a heifer's foot. It navigates the ground
like   catastrophe. There's always shit on the tip. Catch me
befor   e I am hung on the scaffold of dusk, mumbling curses,
seeing   how they taste, thick on the lip, vulgar and salty as cum,
how th   ey creep, quiet and corrupt to the grike of my ear.
I hate my   words. Every second thing is a muttered *cunt*
or *fuck,* a   nd nobody hears (I hope) my strange-dulcet obloquies.
He would h   ave cut me from my mouth, made it somehow sweet.
I forgot how   to go anywhere. Forgot how to dress. He would have
spiked my bra   in, needled me neat. This person I know said
they could unde   rstand, *the gays, Lesbians even* (though
they said it throu   gh the skin of their teeth, all shamed at the saying.
*But the ones who   want both are the worst of all. Something badly
wrong with them, s   hould be shot.* This person I know would have
sent me to him. *Plea   se, Mr Moniz, can you poke the bisexual out?*
And I do wonder. My   own ideates of lust have nothing to do with
tool or cleft. If I want y   ou, it's because I think you are wonderful,
because you made me fe   el like stars, because we'd go together like
beetroot and pixies, becau   se I want to believe in your glorious bones.
If he could have got his ha   nds on me, he would have spired
my socket, left a dream of st   eeples in the corner of my eye.
I would have been sent to him   for the variance, the appetite, the ugly
musings of my skull. He woul   d have cured me with his bright,
amazing knife, done me for a h   usband – meek and muzzled frumpy,
cut me down to a dull sparrow, ha   d me subtle as a wing. He might
have found me already filled with n   ails. Mr Moniz was busy
making us well. Do you know he wo   n the Nobel Prize for breaking
heads? Some quack with a hammer wo   uld have cleaned you from
my cortex. I would not learn your skin's   delicious song. He would have
left no room for angels. Would have pu   nctured me mild as bread.

I am building Paris in my bedroom
Sue Burge

First, I cut a string of paper dolls from a back-copy of *Le Monde* - such a city needs a population of a certain kind of girl. Here's one who arrived in Paris for the first time, shiny, innocent, and left with *je ne sais quoi* and a fringe like Juliette Greco.

I am building Paris in my bedroom. From leftover lego I snap Notre Dame into higgledy shape, balance a flimsy girl on the Quai aux Fleurs. She easily answers the question *Where were you when...?* for she is always in Paris when someone famous dies. She will speak of the friend who died with unwritten dances still inside, how she sat in shock in her Bastille flat, brim with unwept tears.

In my dreams I'm lost in Montreuil's labyrinthine *murs à pêches*, hands a mess of clawed juice, crushed kernel, or I'm deep in the catacombs - conducting a pyramid of skulls grinning dusty harmonies to regretful songs.

I am building Paris in my bedroom. See, here's the Eiffel Tower fashioned from a cat's cradle lifted from my lover's fingers in 1981. Today I plan to craft the silhouette of Sacré Coeur, tear off a wavering girl to place on the steps. She's a girl who had a doll's house but no idea of home; a girl who thinks she sees angels, bought a penny string of beads and named them *rosary*. A girl who looked for love in a scavenged prayerbook.

I am building Paris in my bedroom. Look, I'll put a girl here on Pont St Michel cupping the silk of the Seine like a sacrament to fill her home with light, Gallic shrugs, the joyful lather of French soap, unexpected brioche crumbs between the sofa cushions. This girl knows she's a cliché in her belted mac, angled beret, quick slick of *rouge allure*; some days she is noir to her soul – *resistez, resistez!* A girl can be too cool you know, instead of strutting the streets as if she belongs she should kiss the platform of the Gare du Nord, ecstatic, papal.

I am building Paris in my bedroom. Here are the chaotic market stalls of Barbès clustered under my bed. I fashion them the old way with matchsticks and twine, colour in polystyrene food with felt-tip pens. The trick is to not want to be somewhere else, not to crave the cracked skin of a perfect baguette. This girl, this girl, when she tries to speak her mouth is dry with the rust of unsaid vowels.

43

If You're not Scared
Tessa Foley

Had this idea that one day we'd sit, short-sleeved
along a wall, maybe with a jug of squash, maybe
with a cup of Irish tea, ringing with plain survive
making with life till we fall asleep,
pushing bottles to one side but I come to - it's you
and me and I hiding out in Sunnyside
And you, you put your foot down in the tide,
Well if you're not scared then neither am I.

Had this dream we shattered chalet walls, still
on the beach where parent-bombs with
red cap pockets lie, they haven't even had a drip,
with weary adolescent eyes, we sighed into
the pulsing waves, all swollen with the lies
And in the dream we: you and me and I
could have tombstoned from the sky,
Well if you're not scared to jump, then neither, nor am I.

Had this twinge of sat as three along settee, no white
flang bashing spitting nags but tiptoe tides –
the curtains fading from dark green to light,
You and me and I, we watched
the window as the shore turned to a sheet of ice,
we thought what it is like to be outside, could
have left all snakes and ladders with one roll of the dice,
Well if you're not scared of rolling one, then neither one am I.

Had a second exhalation you and me and I
'd grow up and maybe drive
down to the Dorset coast and see your kids
and mine play in the clearest scum and like in
one, an other life that could be us, run screaming
from each other holding crab legs like a knife, bedraggled,

seaweed swept and making noise their very lives,
But if your kids wouldn't be scared, then pah, neither would mine.

I had one last in mind, your wedding day when I
would shake your wife's warm hand, three cheers and charge
up to a great and mighty age where we'd see skin,
each other's skin unlined, and cast our minds with giggles
back to when sunlight never coughed on any of us twice,
where all the cries were stuffed beneath unsleeping bags,
and up till now, we all have been afraid to die,
but now, if you're not scared, I swear neither am I.

in medias res
RHJ Baker

We will be telling this story years from now
how the beginning had no middle and no end
and arbitrarily we chose the point at which to start talking
in medias res

We will be telling each other
how we cared little for form or matter
gave them shelter
kept them warm

hard by a hovel
somewhere on a heath
somewhere in a storm
that was brewing always
in the distant thunder rumbling
where lightning hardly ever sighted was
heard between effect and cause

We will be telling how we waited bated breath
breathed magic of a stillness that was never silent
never still
always restless
beyond reach
embeckoning
in the voiceless throats of stamens
and the full voiced notes of birds
whose names we never learned

We will be telling how our loud wrung hearts competed with the hammering hail flung f
that was falling all around us in the spring
when the beating cavernousness of catecholamines flooding conscience
came home nothing doing
and the breath stirred moth moralling
before bonfires answered

the first flint struck touch lit flame burnt wood
wagged its weary wings and flew the other way
and no-one good stood up and said
          this will not do this will not wash we will not have you question love

                    We will be telling how we weathered with it
though each dark winter made us doubt
                    how spring could ever muster up her skirts and skip
          through hoops to letter summer's lips with the mystery of a kiss
                    wafting hand lifted from our last farewell shift
          in the last gig we got to when we gigged our way through days
                    beseeming eternity
                    with mind without peace
                    with patience with pain

We will be telling how
when shutters were drawn down and shops went blind
we sat up hackles high knock-kneeing heads together in desire's garret
while busying through pipes our dreams made us make mad monks at prayer
who will turn in despair to opium, psychosis, or religion seem plain

We will be telling how
when the streets were ghosted
the stones in the marketplace were frozen
                    in space
          and space had no meaning till consciousness came
               and shuddered the cart to startle the horse
                    back into lumbering her load up the hill
                    without grudging more than sweat
                    less than steam

          We will be telling how reflection and meditation
               in meditatio omnes populusque tradunt
          the absence of objects and the abundance of space

                         We will be telling how
          when the world awoke to find its feet the other side of the bed

they got up and walked like a leper unlamed
and went forth through walls that had not visioned that space

We will be telling how unfamiliared they felt
when catching wide-eye sidewards glance in car windows
or glass-backed doors
they saw themselves for the first time feelingly
and felt felt fingers invisible their fear for once and for all and
for all their fears

We will be telling how
when the great wheel rolled its way round once more
and we said no no no
no more we can no more bear with this plague no more
it will not wash we will not have you question love
patience patienced pain and brought each patient in the world's weary hospital bread

We will be telling how heaven and earth were more storied than we could
ever dream or hope to know by looking in an almanac
or at an image on a screen
or at the letters littering tetragrammatons in books
that the only tragedy was we could not tell them all
there were so many more than we could ever live have life enough to love

But O how we will say we gloried in the telling of the far flung few we knew
O how we will say the ways in which we spelled out rough and thorough
floured the dough without it needing kneading or
sloughed ours skins each year through drought
bought brougham de villes and rode them to the well
to fill up troughs for our thoroughbreds
while the late choughs' choice electified our voice
as in the closing couplets of the final scenes
when a king has been poisoned
or a prince worried and was shot
without much notice
from a grassy knoll
somewhere in Sarajevo

somewhere in the midst of civil war
somewhere where children are dying

O how we will spell out loud bough brough and borough
cough tough enough and oughta have caught more water
when smooth tooth soothed by floss glossed brushed
were words that washed our mouths from plaque
and pale mirrors red lined irises at night
while dawn drew in the absence of doubt
sighed out our hope

and hell rode by in a handcart to town…

Yakob, you brought me an etrog to give to your mother
Sara Levy

Strange thing. Robust and ugly-beautiful, lovely to its pith and pip, brimful
with ritual. Absurd, to be so canary-vibrant when every cell is halfway dead
click-ticking, tired circadian clock. My etrog sits caged in the colour of itself.

I still don't have the layout of this city, Yakob. Did you take the G train out
to Williamsburg, wander the markets on Wallabout Street, bustle with the
head-scarved bubbehs, the stallholders brandishing their prize fruit *find
something wrong with this!*

I arrive late for Sukkot at your mother's apartment. Your family look on,
puzzled by my roller skates. My red hot pants shed sequins with every
shimmy, I'm balancing a tray of gin & tonics up high, like the table server
swerving through a packed Friday night bar.

Each crystal tumbler is filled with jangling ice and a comedy super-sized slice
of citron. I shout *drink! drink!* to a sea of appalled faces. Your mother faints. I
don't need to speak Yiddish to know everyone is screaming *go home, you've
ruined everything.*

La Buse!
Mehran Waheed

Low above our garden, a rare visitor;
this Common European arrests spring's infected breath,
like a kite teasing us, or
an Airbus from *Blagnac*,
Beluga beak stitching the sky —
blue as a surgical mask.

"La Buse!" my little fledgling cries.

With a gasp
those words unfurl,
rise to pirouette in the air,
spread-eagled like spilled tea,
baby wings eclipsing the inoperable sun.

I course correct her mixed-down tiramisu
feathers, father tongue tied, pulling
creance heartstrings knotted to gloved claw,
but nothing can inoculate me
against the blood clots
translating in my pidgin lungs.

"The buzzard," she perches back, perfectly

immune to nostalgia's
lush birthplace, pleasant breeding land:
binocular-round eyes
enraptured by its deadly embrace,
distant as quarantine,
pangs of hunger opening the gullet
to the vomit of carrion memories.

In that moment, I could have
unhooded the Grim Reaper;
cuffed a luggage tag ring
around the ankle, smuggled
in a kidnapped cuckoo's egg,
sticking to a two-finger arrowhead
formation — just to send us soaring,
strike the longbowman's home.

Leaf Storm
David Butler

i.m. my mother

Some days after the diagnosis
set time, a death-watch beetle,
ticking, you set out undaunted
for the park. Your time of year -
air cold as water, the trees
touched with fleeting majesty.
As we rounded a beech copse,
a puckish wind stirred up and,
like Dante's fugitives, drove all
about a streaming leaf storm,
shoal-dense and endless, brass
after brass, chattering, sheering
in great murmurations, showing
there is raw grandeur in letting go.

Mathematicians Take No Holidays
William Stephenson

The pictures, which yesterday showed haystacks, a kitten
and a Paris café, had melted into random monochrome
blots, decor in the home of a deranged psychiatrist
who'd hired Rorschach as his interior decorator.
Awake before seven, she stared into the stains
that hardened, granular as Pathé newsreel,
as the light built. She reached for her notebook,
sketched stars, epsilons and equalities in 2B pencil.
Her dreams had come in strings of integers for years.

Shingle, still dry at the sea-wall's foot, struck matches
on her trainers. Pulse, one forty. Distance, eight point
seven four k. Her wrist flashed statistics in LED strokes.
The tide's tape-hiss peaked at each breaker into a crest
so rich she inferred a sequence, a SETI astronomer
detecting a waveform so regular it must encode
intelligence, but the signal collapsed into noise
fractal as the tide's filigrees of foam. Logarithms,
chains and domain functions crumbled in her head.

At eight, after a shower, the hotel garden lit up
crystalline. Drops studded twigs, translucent as film.
I'm a husk, she thought, *a shrivelled cocoon, abandoned
to release a theorem after the rain – a mathematical butterfly
projecting patterns onto leaves as its paned wings light them.*
She could barely see the water that brightened her palms
yet she studied them like equations. *A discrete convolution.
Of course.* Like that time a girl questioned her mother
who stood in a corner counting: *Now can I disappear?*

New Language
Vasiliki Albedo

I didn't want that year to be *the year I dropped out,*
so I learnt Mandarin. It went in fits, memorising a few words,
repeating them for days then abandoning it all, only to start again.
Not just the pig and farmer making home, 希望 : xī wàng for hope,
single continuous movements with the brush, syncopating
to the next character. Sometimes they'd appear in my room,
tracing themselves in the air, luminous, starved, manic.
One afternoon I inhabited reckless, 胡, spent three months' salary
tripping down 5th Avenue. Man 人 with a line through
the middle spreads his wings

                                turns into big 大, and I would storm
the Chinese business world. Big with a stroke capping it
becomes the sky 天 you can't exceed, dà xué: big school, what I'd left.
Kāfēi makes it go faster, *worse*, the psychiatrist said, but stack two nights
多 and you have too much work, distracted always by another word,
cycling through the city in harsh weather.
Zì jǐ, alone, menu for the day: 27 clementines, page upon
page of words rushing: 我病了, I feel sick, 最后, most behind,
接收, to accept, and it's about here I detect
a pattern when my notebook, halfway through, comes to a halt.

News from Theia : a Fragment
Steve Xerri

Researchers have found evidence that a planet they have named Theia crashed into the Earth billions of years ago. Traces of the planet have been found during analysis of rocks from the Moon, which may itself have broken out from the collision.

seeing mayflies   usual hatching day   swarms
      dark waters   but this time
    escape velocity proved enough to fling them
past return into the skies, as if their mooring lines
were cut : and that was it – they were not seen again,
their glinting wings, caught briefly in sunlight,
forever gone
          next, the shadows of our birds
thinned out ; bluntheaded owls, the ragged silhouettes
of ravens, all went missing – but we failed to notice
till it was too late
        and then
rain ceased falling on the face of the world
      as cloud streamed off towards the deeps of space
leaving us to dry out, our rivers failing,
our peach and plum trees hung with shrivelled fruits

our sister planet loomed
      suddenly larger in the night, and gleamed
more brightly in her borrowed light, more
        water-washed than ever seen before

there was some talk of making the leap across
      as the favoured twin bore down and wobbled
our rock on its axis, so that clocks went mad
and frosts murdered the summer

I was against it, choosing not to fly
in the gondolas, which duly smashed to pieces
as their airbags tore on the needled peaks
of Earth
    I preferred to stay on land I've loved,
where I am meant to be : now, airstarved
and sick, I await the impact that will grind
this world into the mud of another
          as yet unpeopled
  I etch this message
on a tablet and bury it in the cracked clay
of the pool where I once would watch
the spotted newt swimming with lazy tail-lash,
popping air beads from his mouth

   my atoms now   mind that rode them
    you   these words

Portrait of my Father as a 12th Century Confucian Sage
Ross Cogan

I

For you who were never happy in your own skin
let me paint you another. I will dip the stoat
tail of my brush in sepia ink and coax the stain
into robes appropriate to your age and the shade of year:
black over lambswool, or fawn fur with a white surcoat,
or yellow with fox for winter; for summer wear

a long, bright shirt in linen or course Ge. Then we'll
add trimmings – a sash, a leather belt, edging in silk,
a broad stockade of green fox fur – such signs as will
inform scholars that you are visiting a low
or high official, bereaved female cousin, or the ill
child of a friend. Or perhaps a son returning now

from a long trip away. Let me trim the beard
you grew to hide bad skin, into one more the shape
of that worn by Mencius, the sage. Last, in your hand,
I'll ink a scroll and bamboo pen; place your slippered feet
on an arched bridge over a pool where complaisant carp
circle and baste their mirrored sides in midday heat.

II

Born choking, named for her father by the Jamaican nurse
who thought you'd die before your own parents came back
from their bread-coloured tea, you didn't die, of course.
Yet something of death hung on you like an ill-cut suit,
your own father taken young midway through a joke,
the ash still pacing out his final cigarette.

A stepson taken younger, at night, dying before
the wheels on the upturned car had stopped spinning, a look
of bafflement maturing into mild displeasure.
By then, bullied by the staff at the school you ran,
bullied at home, you'd retired, at first to your book-
clogged room, locked in with Orf's tarot-stained dirges, then

behind your lids, crutched with the fruits of Merck and Pfizer.
Unbolt the door. Step into your new robes, take up
the Analects, take on with it a part where your
basic goodness can be expressed in the right shade
of lambswool and the right words are poised on your lip
ready, and anyway don't always need to be said.

Putty Hill
Matt Hohner

for Kevin

As I ache towards a half-century on Earth, the news
comes in silence first, a social media post, then a phone
call, and only an hour has passed since I was fourteen,
watching *The Breakfast Club* on the VCR, wolfing
down popcorn on Kevin's living room floor in 1985,
licking butter and salt from my fingers, then afterward
his father asking which character each of us resembled.
Kevin and his brother Pat chose the jock and the nerd,
and I answered, *a little of each, but I guess the rebel
because he's angry.* I imagine that same floor where
only a week ago, his mother found him dead, and I think
of his father's shattered heart. I remember how strong
we were in each other, sounding like an approaching storm
on our skateboards as we kicked away at the alley beneath
us, a three-part harmony of urethane, wood, and concrete,
the womb-like soft humidity enveloping our bodies, heat
radiating off the asphalt as the three of us busted new tricks
late into the August night, dripping sweat across the darkness
like signatures, barking shins, skinning elbows and knees,
scraping palms under the parking lot light poles in the office
complex behind their row house. How I savored the cool
wind rippling my soaked t-shirt as I pushed my way home,
blood trickling from new wounds staining my socks while I
picked gravel from the heel of my hand. The braille of raised
scars and dents in my shin bones tells the story of the earned
joy of those boys, those almost-men. We were all gods then.

Reclaim the streets
Hilary Otto

It all started with moss dotting the pavement,
grass edging through the crack between the steps,
shrubs self-seeding and poking out of tiled roofs.

In the distance on the hills across the valley
there's a pine forest. On some days it looked bigger,
but we thought it was just a trick of the haze.

Soon, it got harder to close the front door. Clematis
and jasmine wound their way around the hinges
and sent shoots around the lintel, spreading inside.

One of my friends called to say a sapling had sprouted
in her living room. She had to prune it before she could
watch the telly. It gets worse: apparently it was a sycamore.

Down the road they had a problem with cherry blossom
taking over the entire housing development, invading
each flat one by one like the ants used to way back.

I don't think we'll hold out much longer. I opened
the window this morning to find an enormous hollyhock
blocking my view. It muscled metres high into the air,

its damson-stain flowers raising stamens to the sun
like satellite dishes waiting for a signal. I closed the window,
but tendrils curled around the glass, spiralling out of control.

I called the police, but I think it's too late. Just now I dared
to approach the balcony and saw that the entire street
has turned green, disappeared completely underneath trees.

River Name
Kaozara Oyalowo

I have always been at war with myself, I know how many bullets
are left in the self-destructive gun I purchased in high school.

In the pool changing room, I hung my skin on the chipped blue
hooks along with my uniform & after each class I snaked back

into her with relics I collected of the girls who looked nothing like
me. I imagine myself combing out my ample melanin just after

redirecting my hair to point south rather than north. My mouth,
my nose, my thighs shrinking to hold half of the women I was

moulded from. Instead, I took out a syllable from my river name
which at the time seemed like a worthy sacrifice & I almost died

of thirst. I have always sat in people's mouths awkwardly. Seesaw
tongues throwing me over the bridge of their teeth & I almost - *always* — plunge

to my death. Rescue boats are still crawling the river for my missing
letter. In the news, there are boys missing. Boys that look like my father

when he drives us back to his youth, like a cloud of fumes we enter
his mouth, find the memory he speaks so fondly of, and jump start

our smiles, yes, those boys are missing. Some of the girls too, they say
the water took them, one night they appeared by the water face down.

I know and you probably know too that there is something ominous
about a body not programmed for the sea washing onto the shores,

like when I told my teacher I do not know how to swim well
in my name, she walked me to the pool cliff and when my back

was turned, she pushed me off the edge of her teeth.

Small Mercies
Maeve Henry

After the evening news when despair
trots into the room and rests his heavy
snout upon your lap, pat him gently,
meet his black and burning eyes.
You know you are no Greta. There is
barely a fight left in you, tired woman
with sore feet, sofa warrior; your arrows
are direct debits and petitions, your chariot
of fire, the recycling lorry. This dog may
be descended from Cerberus; still he will
drowse, head heavy on your lap, if you sing
the lullaby of small mercies under your breath:

peat free compost, cloth shopping bags;
loose satsumas, cardboard egg boxes,
electric cars, home-made coffee carried
to the allotment in a flask. Wonky carrots.
Tap water, bamboo socks, recycled bin bags,
moon cups. My children switching off the lights
before they go to bed. My children.

strangers again
Mary Mulholland

My mother said you can't trust people
with an upside-down smile. I didn't listen
and married a man who worked

in trusts and shares, but knew nothing
about trust and sharing. Being lonely
is different to being alone. Sometimes

people you love become strangers.
The stranger of people you once knew
is a different colour to strangers in a crowd.

Strangers I once loved are coloured red.
The chance of bumping into a red stranger
in a crowd is about one in ten thousand.

Then you come towards me in that crowd,
and I want to lose myself. Lost people
in a crowd are only physically present,

they go back to the age of the original sin.
You're laughing, chatting; we're old friends,
you suggest lunch, then I tell you my dream,

how one day a plane dived into my house.
Everyone rushed out to watch it explode,
but it didn't. It just lodged there, like a giant

chimney that didn't work. And you walk away.
A red stranger leaves the after-colour cyan.

(Temper Of) The Swan
Brandon Bennett

The moored boat is long, reflects faintly off the Broads
and I, too tired to remember my fear of water, climb on
nestle into a hole in the bow, a bed, push my scalp into the
       white pillow, coolness dragging me to sleep
and I get used to it, as the nothing days pass, the heron, the tiny fish
the swan, the mallards and their ducks, light breaking through the gaps
to me what is only the warmth on my cheeks is as close dad gets to God.

And I make this blonde friend, who is taller than me – and so is everyone
and spend one fine mooring fishing for nothing
and a few elongated hours fly by, the breeze lifts, the sun slouches
and when at last he catches this thing, this barely fish
       I wonder if he's going to eat it
and he struggles to get it off the hook, his face heated
and he cries, and I am still, and his dad comes and the fish is dead, left
uneaten

And this dad holds him, in his arms, wraps him, his crying child
and I do not know how to think
       and I will never see him again, that kid, as
my father takes us down a different path, a different arm
the Broads wind, widen and contract, timeless and regardless
and we get further and further away from my crying friend and his father
and eventually I will miss them, and eventually I will make myself forget

And this one morning, wrapped in a hoodie, sat on the back of the boat
I watch the waves my dad makes roar into the water
and I watch their tails dissipate
and I obsess over their trajectory, their little lives, their unmarked deaths

And I hunger, as the sun centres, as we come across a raft of ducks
so I sneak into the kitchen and grab this stale white loaf
resume my position, take some for myself, and
       I feed them, the little paddlers, happy for me.

Two great swans join us, and I've heard of their temper
but this audience follows for a while, this regal pair bowing at each
kindly gesture, until eventually I lean over the aft, water still spilling
        into itself, and pet one.

I have never known anyone to pet a swan
        perhaps I am the first, and for as long as I hold my hand there
        it is happy and
at the next pub, I try to tell my dad what happened

But my dad doesn't believe me
and so I don't press it, watch the light through his pint ripple on the wood
and he asks if I want a shandy, and I say yes
                        I want a shandy.

The Fish Shack, Margate
Jane Thomas

Made from poached and patched driftwood
local fish warming their scales on the metal grill
garlic giggling in the pan, sliced tomatoes smiling,
lemons pulped 'n' juiced, marinades of soy and dill.

Local people waiting in line with palms of hot coins
backs turned to the sun, warming in the late of day
backs turned to the bins at the far end of the beach
where shipwrecked nonlocal people kneel and pray.

The Birds
Sharon Black

In their thousands
they occupy the sky until the sun
and all the sea-light is

obliterated. A woman throws
her baby overboard into a stranger's hands,
a man axes his arm

to feed his child.
Each bird's call hangs briefly in the air
before being gulped

by some machinery much greater
than the power plant
along the coast.

This poem is not a song, not a cry for help,
not a paean for the past.
Each feather

fans out like a bouquet
as the thought prepares to land.
Along the beachfront,

lamp-post sentries stare out to sea.
New light makes fallen columns
of the red clay promenade.

I don't know what I hear
when I lie down at night, don't know
what the birds are trying to tell me.

Children tumble from a school bus
without a sound, packs and picnics
jostling. Someone's out there

on a lifeboat, furrowing to shore.
Each thought is sky, thermal
and outstretched body reaching for the ground.

The Minister for Bushfire Recovery is reassigned to Floods

Anne Casey

To our north, a wedding couple watch with
countless millions as their connubial
home drifts slowly down the swollen river,
as fifteen thousand neighbours are evacuated
from their coastal community, where we basked
in beachside sunshine only weeks ago.
To our west, the mountain road I commuted daily
for seven years has slipped into the gully,
closed for the foreseeable future, friends
on either side of the great divide
marooned between mudslides.

Southwest, the city's main dam is spilling
over a year's water supply each day.
Our waterlogged lawn is awash
with motley foliage debris, fat silver
globules shimmering from every
moisture-glutted leaf surface,
fairy-lighting the fringe
of the veranda

where a week ago I watched our dog
stand stock-still for a long while,
gazing out into the distant
skyline as if in praise
of the balmy evening's
languorous descent,
a swoop of sulphur
-crested cockatoo
alighting like
candles in
the waiting gum
(echoed in monstera
blooms flaring out of gloom),

first heralds of an electric
storm brewing in the pinkening
dusk—sub-rosa

presage that this country has more tricks
up its sleeve than the slickest
sideshow illusionist.
Tomorrow, they say,
this pummelling rain will
magically stop and sun
will once again
split rock.

The Daughter's Reckoning
Eve Jackson

This being her last calculation
she made allowances for the 1 son lost
and the wife he'd whittled down to a ½
but not this: the 1 yard
of intolerant leg storming a rocking cot, or the 2 feet
of tubular steel that jerked her Gresham Flyer
and the 4 paces
marched ahead as her stretch of leg multiplied
Or the length of his tongue heard ½ a street
away, or the 2 eyes
that divided her into less than she could be.
Or the years that came with 78s
33 ⅓
45s

that added up to more than teenage years
of usual insecurities as she counted the 18 stairs
obsessively and the 1 door
slammed and locked and checked and locked.
Despite the countless hockey matches missed, 5 sports days
ignored, in adult years, hung on and on 100s of kilometres
of telephone wire. After
subtracting the cost of dutiful drive on the 27
3
25
1
141

she could stop adding up. With no carry-over,
no remainders, so that the 180 degree
arc of arm that carried the 1 kiss
on 2 gloved fingers
to touch the cold marble of skin was the final Total of her
regard for him

72

The Shortest Day
Paul Stephenson

A dark chocolate cake, elegantly displayed,
on an Aubrey Beardsley style vintage plate
by the till in a refurbished coal house café
on the edge of urban wetlands. Where there's
parsnip soup and thick slices of granary bread
for the man who has just ventured inside
to warm himself, after walking the path
that necklaces the inner-city reservoir.

A cold man with a supermarket plastic bag
stuffed inside his jacket pocket, the hole
he's cut with scissors into one of the corners.
An orange plastic bag from the desk drawer
of an upstairs office five miles away, fetched
by another man, suited and softly spoken
who's discreet, keeps a good supply of spares,
advises him on carrying it low to avoid attention.

An orange plastic bag that's full and weighs,
is carried casually, successfully, as though
containing rice or flour or coffee, a bag the man
has been swinging back and forth, back and forth
for half an hour, forty minutes even, longer
than expected, and is, to his relief, not looked at,
not stopped, accused by passers-by, but finding it
physical, the effort needed to make a bag swing.

Swing like incense from an orthodox church
while his legs and feet on autopilot guide him,
glide him around the body of water, its rich border
of reeds and grasses, all biscuit, oatmeal feather,
their dance fashioned by December winds, the bag
buffeted by bluster, bag hitting his knees and shins
as he gets on with swinging, the act of emptying,
happy-go-lucky to those coming the other way.

The everyday swinging of a man wrapped up,
taking in his surroundings, waiting on the spot for
outbreaks of sun, talking aloud, muffled, to someone,
describing a spire in the distance, all the way round
before stopping to turn, head back to the warmth
of the coal house, him arriving shaken out, him
lighter and hungry, denim shins and winter shoes
dusted like icing sugar on a dark chocolate cake.

Unbridled

Alexandra Corrin-Tachibana

*As long as she thinks of a man, nobody objects to a woman thinking' —*Virginia Woolf

I'm thinking of Andrea McLean —
I cried when she left *Loose Women*,
how openly she spoke of loneliness

in a marriage. My thoughts turn to
our beach wedding: you and me,
and an expenses spreadsheet.

We wore Hawaiian leis. Auntie
Anne watched the DVD, said it was
like 'An Officer and a Gentleman'.

I remember you covered my mouth
when I came.

I'm in a poetry workshop with Jack
Underwood: patterns in language –
– *the tyranny of the habitual*, how

dull it can be, our tendency to talk
of a *line of trees*. I think of the quote
from Gibran about the cypress and

the oak, failing to grow in each
other's shadow; and of the scold's
bridle to tame women. Since I told

you I don't love you anymore,
you've taken up gardening. My
birth flower is a pink rose —

for happiness.

I'm on the phone to Dad before
Corrie. He says the affair between
Alina and Tyrone is ridiculous –

when she says let me show you
how much I love you. As if it's that
simple.

I say, 'I'll let you get back to your
Corrie'. And wonder why you
encouraged me to debate at Oxford,

but not to speak up about day-to-
day stuff. I recall you say: *he's from*
a different culture; *had a difficult*

childhood. You remind me of what
Granny Corrin used to say: *don't*
shit in your own nest.

And I think of the witch's bridle —
a cage for the head — to silence
women.

But then there's you, G. — our
WhatsApp routine — the joking
about my Couch to 5K, on the

bridleway. You're imagining
runaway brides in wedding gowns
and I'm telling you how freely the

horses stomp about. Unrestrained,
uncontainable. And I think of TV's
Miranda, how she says women

should make galloping a thing,
should gallop through shopping
malls. I picture her.

Galloping along for all that she's
worth. Mouth hanging open.

Untying the Rat King
Jonathan Greenhause

Cynthia shushes the oinking mud-encrusted pig in his wicker basket,
offers a stale biscuit from her left hand missing its pinky

ever since the threshing mishap. Gerald, middle-aged, stares askew,
inquires who invited her to this clandestine

Death Match between local farm boy
& local farm boy. "Local farm boy killed my dad," Cynthia seethes,

not mentioning which of the two. Gerald knows nothing about truth,
thus assumes she's telling it. His explosive demise

will arrive in an upscale box, his life a series
of staggered postponements of the inevitable. Endangered butterflies

jam the vestibule, flit in & out of sunlit dust motes,
as a Bengal tiger snoozes, chained to a grinning toothless old man

sunk into a rocking chair. A rickety lift shudders into movement
before plummeting into the shaft's darkness

where a rat king painstakingly tries untying its knotted link to royalty,
dozens of vermin stuck to the porous border

between independence & power. Cynthia soon slips
into an all-male crowd, sets her pig loose, the initial shock of his squeals

leading to a stamping of toes, elbows jabbing irritable wagers,
a flurry of fisticuffs, then a lightning flash of blinding fluorescence

leaping off a polished blade, a convex belly
opening like a blossomed flower, this human stampede's spill

a carton of milk with a bullet shot through. Cynthia snatches her pig,
unwraps her boyfriend's roped wrists. "How'd you find me?!"

he shouts as they bound up a back stairwell, past the bison,
atop which a dozing girl grasps its curled tufts of fur

as she dreams of prairies ceding to a rolling ocean of floating plastic.
"I listened to the wind," she whispers, shoots the tiger

with a tranquilizer, hands the old man a package
of dentures encased in gold, payment for their Greyhound ticket

out of this local farmland, where their epitaphs were inscribed,
were just waiting for them to entangle their tails with everyone else's.

water music
Gillie Robic

the water was clear and rising
I gave up looking for my shoes
floating among the others
or maybe not
maybe sunk to the bottom
paired modestly on the pavement
as if waiting for a bus
or a submarine

the water was clear and rising
the temperature perfect
I gave up searching the side streets
forgot what it was I was looking for
and swam towards Warren Street Station
wondering how the water would travel
underground finding its own level
of course

the water was clear and rising
strangely free of flotsam and jetsam
just the occasional briefcase
and one or two bags for life
there was a flash of silver
a shoal of small fish darted out
and turned towards
Euston Road

the water was clear and rising
through the underpass flowing
into the glassy entrances of UCH
where nurses and orderlies smiled
and paddled and doctors floated
on their backs watching cloud formations
and the empty towering skyline
scraping the blue

the water was clear and rising
I could no longer resist the pull
so I duck-dived into the sunlit depths
peering through first-floor windows
at abandoned IT and forests of paper
undulating in the gentle currents
pot plants rotating off the desks
towards the ceiling.

the water was clear and rising
with all sorts of useless debris
from outlets on the ground floor
perfume and packaged razors
scented candles craft beer
high-end handbags Jimmy Choos
which reminded me I had been looking
for my flip-flops a life-time ago

the water was clear and rising
I descended into commercial penumbra
but nothing looked like something
I would need drifting peacefully
down Tottenham Court Road
to Soho and Theatre Land checking out
empty auditoriums lighting rigs
swaying over broken stages

the water was clear and rising
I dived to the Cenotaph
saluted the glorious dead
hung like Harold Lloyd on the arms of Big Ben
looked down on the Mother of Parliaments
before letting go to old Father Thames
sweeping through bridges and barriers
past supermarket trolleys and sunken hulks

out to the estuary
wide as the sea
the familiar ocean
rising overhead
children playing
in their element
arching like dolphins
into the air

You're The Boy with a Gun in His Bedroom
Stuart Charlesworth

Turn your attention to the wardrobe.
        Do you see how those white doors
mark it as different, as not belonging
        to you? To open them
(as you'll do now) allows a parental presence
        to enter your space.

Inside, there are:
        blankets (folded neatly)
photograph albums, account books and folders
        and hiding underneath them
in a shoebox is the gun
        and an aspirin container filled with bullets.

When you pick up the gun
        don't point it or wave it around.
Know that it is not one of your toys.
        be aware of the weight of it
large in your hands, but do not examine
        the short barrel closely —

to start to think how
        a slaughter-man's gun
does not need to propel
        the slug accurately,
as it's pressed to the side
        of the animal's head

will make an Alice of you.
        The room will distort,
you'll weaken and swoon
        as you sprout
to a size far too large.
        Instead, use childish wits

on the child-proof cap
      of the aspirin bottle.
Pop it off, and watch
      the bright-painted rounds pour out;
feel how the grooves in their ends
      draw to an ice-cream cone tip.

Then, run to the window
      stand barefoot on the sill
and cling to the frame;
      place your ear by the open uppermost pane
and listen to the bark of shotguns
      echoing across the village.